The Royal Court
presents

ATTEMPTS ON HER LIFE

by Martin Crimp

First performance at the
Royal Court Theatre Upstairs, West Street 7 March 1997.

faber and faber
LONDON · BOSTON

The Royal Court Theatre is financially assisted by the Royal
Borough of Kensington and Chelsea. Recipient of a grant from
the Theatre Restoration Fund & from the Foundation for Sport
& the Arts. The Royal Court's Play Development Programme
is funded by the Audrey Skirball-Kenis Theatre. Supported by
the National Lottery through the Arts Council of England.
Royal Court Registered Charity number 231242.

The English Stage Company at the Royal Court Theatre

The English Stage Company was formed to bring serious writing back to the stage. The first Artistic Director, George Devine, wanted to create a vital and popular theatre. He encouraged new writing that explored subjects drawn from contemporary life as well as pursuing European plays and forgotten classics. When John Osborne's **Look Back in Anger** was first produced in 1956, it forced British Theatre into the modern age. In addition to plays by "angry young men", the international repertoire ranged from Brecht to Ionesco, by way of Jean Paul Sartre, Marguerite Duras, Wedekind and Beckett.

The ambition was to discover new work which was challenging, innovative and also of the highest quality, underpinned by the desire to discover a contemporary style of presentation. Early Court writers included Arnold Wesker, John Arden, David Storey, Ann Jellicoe, N F Simpson and Edward Bond. They were followed by David Hare and Howard Brenton, Caryl Churchill, Timberlake Wertenbaker, Robert Holman and Jim Cartwright. Many of their plays are now regarded as modern classics.

Many established playwrights had their early plays produced in the Theatre Upstairs including Anne Devlin, Andrea Dunbar, Sarah Daniels, Jim Cartwright, Clare McIntyre, Winsome Pinnock, Martin Crimp and Phyllis Nagy. Since 1994 there has been a major season of plays by writers new to the Royal Court, many of them first plays, produced in association with the *Royal National Theatre Studio* with sponsorship from *The Jerwood Foundation*. The writers include Joe Penhall, Nick Grosso, Judy Upton, Sarah Kane, Michael Wynne, Judith Johnson, James Stock, Simon Block and Mark Ravenhill. In 1996-97 The Jerwood Foundation sponsored the Jerwood New Playwrights season, a series of six plays by Jez Butterwoth and Martin McDonagh (in the Theatre Downstairs), Mark Ravenhill, Ayub Khan-Din, Tamantha Hammerschlag and Jess Walters (in the Theatre Upstairs).

Theatre Upstairs productions have regularly transferred to the Theatre Downstairs, as with Ariel Dorfman's **Death and the Maiden**, Sebastian Barry's **The Steward of Christendom**, a co-production with *Out of Joint*, and Martin McDonagh's **The Beauty Queen Of Leenane,** a co-production with Druid Theatre Company. Some Theatre Upstairs productions have transferred to the West End, most recently with Kevin Elyot's **My Night With Reg** at the Criterion.

1992-1996 have been record-breaking years at the box-office with capacity houses for productions of **Faith Healer**, **Death and the Maiden**, **Six Degrees of Separation**, **King Lear**, **Oleanna**, **Hysteria**, **Cavalcaders**, **The Kitchen**, **The Queen & I**, **The Libertine**, **Simpatico**, **Mojo** and **The Steward of Christendom**.

Death and the Maiden and **Six Degrees of Separation** won the Olivier Award for Best Play in 1992 and 1993 respectively. **Hysteria** won the 1994 Olivier Award for Best Comedy, and also the Writers' Guild Award for Best West End Play. **My Night with Reg** won the 1994 Writers' Guild Award for Best Fringe Play, the Evening Standard Award for Best Comedy, and the 1994 Olivier Award for Best Comedy. Jonathan Harvey won the 1994 Evening Standard Drama Award for Most Promising Playwright, for **Babies**. Sebastian Barry won the 1995 Writers' Guild Award for Best Fringe Play for **The Steward of Christendom** and also the 1995 Lloyds Private Banking Playwright of the Year Award. Jez Butterworth won the 1995 George Devine Award for Most Promising Playwright, the 1995 Writers' Guild New Writer of the Year, the Evening Standard Award for Most Promising Newcomer and the 1995 Olivier Award for Best Comedy for **Mojo**. Phyllis Nagy won the 1995 Writers' Guild Award for Best Regional Play for **Disappeared**. Martin McDonagh won the 1996 George Devine Award for Most Promising Playwright, the 1996 Writers' Guild Best Fringe Play Award, and the 1996 Evening Standard Drama Award for Most promising Newcomer for **The Beauty Queen of Leenane**. The Royal Court won the 1995 Prudential Award for the Theatre, and was the overall winner of the 1995 Prudential Award for the Arts for creativity, excellence, innovation and accessibility. The Royal Court won the 1995 Peter Brook Empty Space Award for innovation and excellence in theatre.

Now in its temporary homes The Duke Of York's and Ambassadors Theatres, during the two-year refurbishment of its Sloane Square theatre, the Royal Court continues to present the best in new work. After four decades the company's aims remain consistent with those established by George Devine. The Royal Court is still a major focus in the country for the production of new work. Scores of plays first seen at the Royal Court are now part of the national and international dramatic repertoire.

How the Royal Court is brought to you

The Royal Court (English Stage Company Ltd) is supported financially by a wide range of public bodies and private companies, as well as its own trading activities. The company receives its principal funding from the **Arts Council of England**, which has supported the Royal Court since 1956. The **Royal Borough of Kensington & Chelsea** gives an annual grant to the Royal Court Young People's Theatre. The **London Boroughs Grants Committee** contributes to the cost of productions in the Theatre Upstairs.

Other parts of the company's activities are made possible by business sponsorships. Several of these sponsors have made a long-term commitment. 1996 saw the sixth Barclays New Stages Festival of Independent Theatre, supported throughout by **Barclays Bank**. **British Gas North Thames** supported three years of the Royal Court's Education Programme. Sponsorship by **WH Smith** helped to make the launch of the Friends of the Royal Court scheme so successful.

1993 saw the start of our association with the **Audrey Skirball-Kenis Theatre** of Los Angeles, which is funding a Playwrights Programme at the Royal Court. Exchange visits for writers between Britain and the USA complement the greatly increased programme of readings and play development which have fortified the company's capability to develop writing for the theatre nationally and internationally.

In 1988 the **Olivier Building Appeal** was launched, to raise funds to begin the task of restoring, repairing and improving the Royal Court Theatre, Sloane Square. This was made possible by a large number of generous supporters and significant contributions from the **Theatres Restoration Fund**, the **Rayne Foundation**, the **Foundation for Sport and the Arts** and the **Arts Council's Incentive Funding Scheme**.

The Company earns the rest of the money it needs to operate from the Box Office, from other trading and from transfers to the West End of plays such as **Death and the Maiden**, **Six Degrees of Separation**, **Oleanna** and **My Night With Reg**. But without public subsidy it would close immediately and its unique place in British theatre would be lost. If you care about the future of arts in this country, please write to your MP and say so.

At the Royal Court Theatre Downstairs
St. Martin's Lane WC2

The Royal Court Theatre presents

From 13 February

THE SHALLOW END
by Doug Lucie

The Royal Court Theatre presents
From 10 April   AT&T: *OnStage*

THE WAKE
by Tom Murphy

The Royal Court, Tamasha Theatre Company and Birmingham Repertory Theatre present

From 28 May

EAST IS EAST
by Ayub Khan-Din

At the Royal Court Theatre Upstairs
West St WC2

8 - 12 April

VOICES FROM SPAIN

A week of new plays, translated into English, from Spanish and Catalan.

ATTEMPTS ON HER LIFE

by Martin Crimp

Cast (in alphabetical order)

Kacey Ainsworth

Danny Cerqueira

David Fielder

Ashley Jensen

Hakeem Kae-Kazim

Etela Pardo

Sandra Voe

Howard Ward

Director	Tim Albery
Designer	Gideon Davey
Lighting Designer	Simon Mills
Sound Designer	Paul Arditti
Production Manager	Paul Handley
Senior Stage Manager	Maris Sharp
Stage Managers	Katy Hastings
	Simon Wilcock
	Helen Bond
Costume Supervisor	Sam Mealing
Assistant Director	Rufus Norris
Composition	David Benke
Movement	Patti Powell
Video/Photographic Imagery	Jackie Oudney

The Royal Court would like to thank the following for their help with this production: Extreme Facilities Ltd; Wardrobe care by Persil and Comfort courtesy of Lever Brothers Ltd, refrigerators by Electrolux and Philips Major Appliances Ltd.; kettles for rehearsals by Morphy Richards; video for casting purposes by Hitachi; backstage coffee machine by West 9; furniture by Knoll International; freezer for backstage use supplied by Zanussi Ltd 'Now that's a good idea.' Hair styling by Carole at Moreno, 2 Holbein Place, Sloane Square 0171- 730- 0211; Closed circuit TV cameras and monitors by Mitsubishi UK Ltd. Natural spring water from Wye Spring Water, 149 Sloane Street, London SW1, tel. 0171-730 6977. Overhead projector from W.H. Smith; Sanyo U.K for the backstage microwave.

Martin Crimp (writer)
For the Royal Court:
The Treatment (winner of
the 1993 John Whiting
Award), No One Sees the
Video, Getting
Attention(West Yorkshire
Playhouse Production).
Other theatre includes:
Four Attempted Acts,
Definitely the Bahamas,
Play with Repeats,
Dealing with Clair
(Orange Tree), and a
contemporary adaptation
of The Misanthrope
(Young Vic).
Forthcoming projects
include translations of
Roberto Zucco and
Ionesco's The Chairs, and
a film adaptation of
Dealing with Clair.
Martin is currently Writer
in Residence at the Royal
Court.

Tim Albery (director)
Theatre includes: Krapp's
Last Tape, Kennedy's
Children, Oh Coward!,
Confusions, Statements
After an Arrest, Jumpers,
(Liverpool Playhouse);
Ellen Cassidy (Liverpool
Everyman); The Man
Himself (Orange Tree,
Richmond); Waiting
For Godot (Contact,
Manchester); Machine
Wreckers (Half Moon,
London); Ella, War
Crimes, Princess of
Cleves (ICA, London);
Paradise, Women Beware
Women (Avon Touring,
Bristol); Abigail's Party
(Essen, West Germany);
Heartbreak House
(Göttingen, West
Germany); Venice
Preserved, Hedda Gabler

(Almeida, London); Secret
Gardens (Mickery,
Amsterdam & ICA);
New Tactics (Second
Stride); Under Western
Eyes (Ro, Amsterdam);
Insignificance (Oxford
Theatre Co.); A Street
Car Named Desire
(Crucible, Sheffield);
Mary Stuart (Greenwich
Theatre); As You Like
It (Old Vic); Berenice
(RNT); Wallenstein,
Macbeth (RSC).
Opera includes:
The Turn of the Screw
(Batiguano, Italy);
Mozart at Palm Springs
(The Place, London);
Don Giovanni, La Finta
Giardinera, Don Carlos,
Luisa Miller (Opera
North); The Midsummer
Marriage (Opera North &
Scottish Opera); The
Trojans (Opera North,
Welsh National Opera,
Opera de Nice & Scottish
Opera); The Rape of
Lucretia (Goteborg,
Sweden); Billy Budd,
Beatrice and Benedict,
Lohengrin (ENO); Peter
Grimes (ENO & Bavarian
State Opera); La Wally
(Bregenz Festival Opera);
Cherubin (ROH); Fidelio
(Scottish Opera);Nabucco
(Welsh National Opera
& ROH); Simon
Boccanegra, Ariadne
Auf Naxos (Bavarian
State Opera); A
Midsummer Night's
Dream (Metropolitan
Opera, New York).
Television: Dancehouse
Four.

Kacey Ainsworth
For the Royal Court:
Pale Horse.
Other theatre includes:
The Boys From Syracuse,
The Merchant of Venice
(Harrogate Theatre);
Serving it Up (Bush
Theatre).
Television includes:
The Moonstone, Cone
Zone, Accused, The Bill,
A Touch of Frost, No
Bananas, Soldier Soldier,
Under the Moon, Peak
Practice.
Radio: Taking Pictures.

Paul Arditti
(sound design)
For the Royal Court work
includes:The Shallow
End, Shopping and
F***ing (and Out
of Joint); The Lights, The
Thickness of Skin,
Sweetheart, Bruises, Pale
Horse, The Changing
Room, Hysteria, Rat in
the Skull (Royal Court
Classics), The Steward of
Christendom (and
Out of Joint), Mojo,
Simpatico, The Strip,
Blasted, Peaches,
Some Voices,
My Night with Reg,
The Kitchen, Search
and Destroy.
Other theatre sound
design includes:
As You Like It (RSC);
Tartuffe (Manchester
Royal Exchange); The
Threepenny Opera
(Donmar Warehouse);
Hamlet (Gielgud); Piaf
(Piccadilly); St. Joan
(Strand & Sydney Opera
House); The Trackers
of Oxyrhynchus (RNT);
The Gift of the Gorgon

(RSC); *Orpheus Descending (Theatre Royal, Haymarket & Broadway); The Merchant of Venice (Phoenix & Broadway); A Streetcar Named Desire (Bristol Old Vic); Matador (Queens); The Rose Tattoo (Playhouse); Becket, Cyrano de Bergerac (Theatre Royal, Haymarket); Travesties (Savoy); Four Baboons Adoring the Sun (Lincoln Center, 1992 Drama Desk Award).*

David Benke *(composer)* Composer and lecturer. Interests lie in working collaboratively in the forms of dance, film and theatre. Worked with Primitive Science on two productions at the Young Vic, *Spell* and *Imperfect Librarian*. Video/Sound project 556459 won Jury Prize at 1996 ACREQ Electro-Video Clip Awards (Canada): *String Quartet Ungestum* received Purcell Room Premiere and his quintet gained first prize in the 1993 Royal Over-Seas League competition.

Daniel Cerqueira Theatre includes: *The Art of Random Whistling (Wink productions/Young Vic); Antony and Cleopatra (Moving Theatre international tour); Crocodile Looking at Birds (Lyric Hammersmith; Days of Hope (Hampstead).*

Television includes: Hot Dog Wars. *Film includes: Valley Girls, Method in Madness.*

Gideon Davey *(designer)* Recent design for theatre includes: *A Doll's House (New End Theatre); Fatzer (Gate, Nominated Best Design London Fringe Awards); Song at Twilight (Greenwich); Love on the Dole (Maridians); Great Expectations (Salisbury); Night Must Fall (Windosr); Macbeth (Sheffield Crucible).* Design for opera includes: *Peter Grimes (Cambridge); Macbeth (City of Birmingham Touring Opera); Faust (Costume design, Volksoper Vienna).* Gideon trained at Bath Academy of Art, Nottingjham Polytechnic and was a Linbury Prize finalist.

David Fielder For the Royal Court: *Uganda, The Break of Day, The Three Sisters (and Out of Joint), Not Quite Jerusalem, Panic.* Other theatre includes: *Trafford Tanzi (Mermaid); The Choice (Salisbury); Trilby (adaptation for Shared Experience); Richard II (Royal Exchange, Manchester); Lear (Talawa Arts); Twelfth Night (Salisbury, Edinburgh, & tour of China); War and Peace (RNT); Paper Husband*

(Hampstead); Beginning to End (Toronto). Television includes: *The Naked Civil Servant, Inspector Morse, Spatz, Widows, The Bill.* Films include: *Yanks, Superman III, The Pledge.*

Ashley Jensen For the Royal Court: *Storming, Uganda.* Other theatre includes: *The Architect (Traverse Theatre); The Big Picnic (Bill Bryden ,Glasgow); The Prime of Miss Jean Brodie (Lyceum, Edinburgh); The Guid Sisters, The Real Wurld ?, Salvation, The Treasure of Wookimagoo, The Witches of Pollok (Tron Theatre, Glasgow); The Crucible, The Snow Queen (Glasgow Citizens); Rab C. Nesbitt (Phil McIntyre Productions); The Resistable Rise of Arturo Ui (7.84 Glasgow); Mandy Redmayne Steps into a Story (Pocket Theatre); Oor Wullie (Jimmy Logan's Company); Carluccio and the Queen of Hearts (Fifth Estate Edinburgh).* Television includes: *Bad Boys, Capital Lives, Waiting, Roughnecks, The Bill, May to December, Taking Over the Asylum, Para Handy, Down Among the Big Boys, Rab C Nesbitt, City Lights, Dreaming, Tickets for the Zoo,.*

Hakeem Kae-Kazim
For the Royal Court:
The Lights.
Other theatre includes:
Indigo, The Merchant
of Venice, Julius Caesar,
Measure for Measure
(RSC); King Lear,
Richard III (RNT);
Othello, Henry V
(National Youth Theatre);
Macbeth (Theatr Clwyd,
U.S tour and Bridge
Lane Theatre, London);
Say Zebra (Gate
Theatre, London); The
Rover (Women's
Playhouse Trust).
Television includes:
Trial and Retribution,
The Bill, Alive and
Kicking, Runaway Bay,
The 90 Days Pub, Grease
Monkeys, Grange Hill,
Ellington, The Rover,
Julius Caesar.
Film: Double Vision,
Sumner's Drop.
Radio: Arts and Africa,
An Inspector Calls,
Curse of the Water
Hyacinth, A Midsummer
Night's Dream.

Simon Mills (lighting)
Theatre includes:
Waiting for Godot,
Accidental Death of an
Anarchist, Hansel and
Gretel, Romeo and Juliet,
Ay Carmella, Generations
of the Dead in the Abyss
of Coney Island Madness
(Contact, Manchester);
Nest of Spies (Northern
Stage); Song at Twilight
(Greenwich); The
Weavers (Gate); A
Doll's House, Barnaby
Downing (New End);
Born Bad, Chelsea
Girls Man in the Moon);

Seeing Marie, The
Impressario of
Smyrna, What Do I Get
(Old Red Lion).
Opera includes:
La Boheme (Scottish
Opera); The Marriage
of Figaro (Mid Wales
opera); Susannah
(Birmingham Millennium
Festival); Dr Miracle ,
L'Enfant et Les Sortileges
(Birmingham
Conservatoire); Gulliver
(Malvern Festival);
Marriage of Figaro
(Opera Bravo); Il
Travatore (Holland
Park); Eugene Onegin
(Co Opera).

Etela Pardo
Theatre includes:
The Ends of the Earth
(RNT); Antony and
Cleopatra (Riverside
Studios); Agammenon's
Children (The Gate); A
Doll's House, Three
Sisters, The Brothers
Karamazov, Tales
From Vienna Woods,
Ivanov, Lear, The
Wood (Sarajevo
National Theatre).
Television includes:
Young Freud, Diary of
the Milic Family, War,
Simha, Birdcage
(Sarajevo TV)
Films: Valter Defends
Sarajevo, Defiance,
The Saint.

Sandra Voe
For the Royal Court:
The Kitchen.
Other recent theatre
includes: The Winter
Guest (Almeida); Trouble
Sleeping(Warehouse);The
Deep Blue Sea (Almeida

and Apollo); A Delicate
Balance (Nottingham);
Medea (Royal Exchange);
The Birthday Party
(Shared Experience tour);
The Strangeness of Others
(RNT).
Television includes:
Holding On, Hello Girls,
Bare Necessities, A
Village Affair, Body and
Soul, The Crying Game,
Love Hurts, Uncle Vanya,
Changing Step, Donal and
Sally, Stepping Out, Ruth
Rendell Mysteries.
Film includes: Agatha,
The Ploughman's Lunch,
Local Hero, Comrades,
Immortal Beloved,
Breaking the Waves, The
Winter Guest.

Howard Ward
For the Royal Court:
Pale Horse.
Other theatre includes:
work at many provincial
theatres, and long seasons
at both the RSC and the
RNT, and most recently
was in King Arthur (Paris/
London).
Television includes:
Insiders, EastEnders,
Radio: He has recently
directed two 90 minutes
plays for radio.

Stage Hands Appeal

Royal Court Theatre

Many thanks to everyone who has supported the Stage Hands appeal so far. Our goal, to raise over £500,000 from friends and audience members toward the £16 million redevelopment of the Royal Court Theatre, Sloane Square, has already raised £160,000 - a great start.

A special thank you to everyone who is supporting us with covenanted donations: covenants are particularly important because we can claim back the tax a donor has already paid, which increases the value of the donation by *over one third* (at no extra cost to the donor). The same applies to Gift Aid, which adds one third to the value of all single donations of £250 or more. It is vital we make the most of all our donations so if you're able to make a covenanted contribution to the theatre's Stage Hands Appeal please call 0171-930-4253.

A MODEL THEATRE

You've seen the show, read the playtext and eaten the ice-cream - but what to do with all the loose change left over from the evening's entertainment? The Royal Court's 'Model Money Box' may be just the answer. The money box is a replica model of the new-look Royal Court, complete with undercroft cafe, new circle bar balcony and re-shaped auditorium. Notes and coins gratefully received.

BUILDING UPDATE

Both our Lottery grant and partnership funding are hard at work for us now as the Redevelopment in Sloane Square continues apace. With the stripping out-process almost complete, and the stage, seats, fixtures and fittings all removed, we can start to get down to the project's three 'Rs'; Re-structuring, Re-building and Refurbishing.

Hoardings will shortly be going up around the front of the theatre, securing the site and providing building access, which means that the much-loved Royal Court Theatre facade will disappear from view for a while. However, out-of-sight (or should that be site?) is definitely not out-of-mind and a photo display in the Theatre Downstairs lobby will provide building updates as the work progresses.

Stage Hands Appeal

ROYAL COURT DIARY

The Porchester Hall in Queensway, once notorious for its drag balls and Turkish baths, was the venue for the Royal Court's recent 40th Anniversary gala, hosted by The New Yorker and Hugo Boss.

The centrepiece of this glittering evening was a cabaret directed by the Court's Artistic Director, Stephen Daldry, and as the 450 diners laid down their silverware an explosion shook the room and thirty chefs and waitresses from Arnold Wesker's *The Kitchen* burst onto the stage. But it wasn't just the cast from *The Kitchen* and David Storey's *The Changing Room* who provided the entertainment: Jeremy Irons' rendition of a piece from Christopher Hampton's *Savages*, backed by authentic South American musicians, hushed the room; Sloane Square favourites Kens Cranham and Campbell performed a piece from *Waiting for Godot*; Harriet Walter re-created her role from Timberlake Wertenbaker's *Three Birds Alighting on a Field*, offering a hilarious portrait of the socialite finding salvation through art; and Stephen Fry delivered PG Wodehouse's wonderful poem, *The Audience at the Court Theatre*.

Famous faces including Melvyn Bragg, Nigel Hawthorne, Helen Mirren, Ruby Wax, Salman Rushdie, Mick Jagger, Jerry Hall and Vanessa Redgrave were thrilled by the theatrical magic of the evening and the money raised by the gala will play an important part in getting the redevelopment work in Sloane Square off the ground.

TAKE YOUR SEATS

There will be almost 400 new seats in the refurbished Theatre Downstairs and over 60 in the Theatre Upstairs - all of which are offered 'for sale'. Not only will the seats in the Theatre Downstairs have the printed name of the seat's 'owner', they will also bear the owner's *signature*. Seats may be bought on behalf of children and grandchildren and can be signed by the children themselves. Companies are also eligible to take part in the scheme and their business logos will printed on the plaques.

For details of the 'Take A Seat' scheme please call 0171-930-4253.

STAGE HANDS T-SHIRTS

Stage Hands T-shirts are now on sale at the Bookshop in the Theatre Downstairs and in the bar at the Theatre Upstairs, price £10.

For futher details about Stage Hands and the

Redevelopment

please call the

Development Office

on 0171-930-4253

Royal Court Theatre

For the Royal Court

Attempts on her Life

First published in 1997
by Faber and Faber Limited
3 Queen Square London WC1N 3AU

Typeset by Faber and Faber Ltd
Printed in England by Mackays of Chatham plc, Chatham, Kent

A CIP record for this book
is available from the British Library

ISBN 0-571-19215-7

2 4 6 8 10 9 7 5 3 1

17 SCENARIOS FOR THE THEATRE

1 ALL MESSAGES DELETED
2 TRAGEDY OF LOVE AND IDEOLOGY
3 FAITH IN OURSELVES
4 THE OCCUPIER
5 THE CAMERA LOVES YOU
6 MUM AND DAD
7 THE NEW ANNY
8 PARTICLE PHYSICS
9 THE THREAT OF INTERNATIONAL TERRORISM™
10 KINDA FUNNY
11 UNTITLED (100 WORDS)
12 STRANGELY!
13 JUNGFRAU (WORD ASSOCIATION)
14 THE GIRL NEXT DOOR
15 THE STATEMENT
16 PORNÓ
17 PREVIOUSLY FROZEN

This is a piece for a company of actors whose composition should reflect the composition of the world beyond the theatre.

Let each scenario in words – the dialogue – unfold against a distinct world – a design – which best exposes its irony.

A dash (–) at the beginning of a line indicates a change of speaker. If there is no dash after a pause, it means the same character is still speaking.

A slash (/) marks the point of interruption in overlapping dialogue.

beep

—Anne. (*pause*) It's me. (*pause*) I'm calling from Vienna.
(*pause*) No, sorry, I'm calling from . . . Prague. (*pause*)
It's Prague. (*pause*) I'm pretty sure it's Prague. Anyway,
look . . . (*breath*) Anne . . . (*breath*) I want to apolo-
gize. (*breath*) I realize how much I've hurt you, my
sweet sweet darling, and . . . (*breath*) Ah. Look. Look,
there's somebody on the other line, Anne. I really really
– I'm sorry – but I really really have to take this call.
I'll get back to you.

'*Monday 8.53 a.m.*'

beep

—Anne. Hi. Listen. I only have a moment. Are you there?
No? Okay. Look. It's this. What we were discussing?
You remember? Well what about this, what about this,
what about if, let's say, let's say, let's just say . . . that the
trees have names? Okay? That's right – the trees. You
think – I know – you think I'm crazy. But let's just
accept for a moment shall we that the trees have names.
Then what if, what if, what about if . . . *this was her
tree*. Shit. Sorry. Look, I have to board now. But think
about that. The trees have names. And one of them is
hers. I have to run.

'*Monday 9.35 a.m.*'

beep

— (*spoken in e.g. Czech*) You know who this is. You
leave the device in a small truck at the back of the
building. You'll get the truck from Barry. Barry will
contact you with more instructions.

'*Monday 11.51 a.m.*'

— . . . Oh. Hello? It's Mum . . .

'Monday 1.05 p.m.'

beep

—Hello, this is Sally at Coopers. Just to let you know that the vehicle *is* now in the showroom and ready for your collection. Thank you.

'Monday 1.06 p.m.'

beep

—We know where you live you fucking bitch. You're dead, basically. The things you fucking did. We don't forget. (*pause*) You'll wish you'd never been *born*.

'Monday 1.32 p.m.'

beep

— . . . Anne? Hello? It's Mum again. (*pause*) Got your postcard. (*pause*) Looks very nice. (*pause*) And the photo. Is that really you? (*pause*) Glad you're making friends and so on. (*pause*) The thing is, Anne, there just isn't any money to send you. I've spoken to your Dad, and he says no, absolutely not.
(*We hear a man's voice in the background: 'Not another penny. Just you make that clear.' Mum replies: 'I'm telling her, I'm telling her.' Then back into the phone.*)
I'm really sorry, Anne darling, but we just can't keep on doing it.
(*Man's voice again: 'If you don't tell her, I'll bloody well talk to her.'*)
Look, I have to go now, darling. Your Dad sends his love. All right? God bless.

'Monday 2.20 p.m.'

2

—Anne? Are you there? Pick up the phone, Annie. (*pause*)
Okay . . . It's a quarter after ten here in Minnesota and
we're just calling to say our thoughts and prayers are
with you, Annie. And we love you very much.

'*Monday 4.13 p.m.*'

—Anne? Brilliant. It's moving. It's timely. It's distressing.
It's funny. It's sexy. It's deeply serious. It's entertaining.
It's illuminating. It's cryptic. It's dark. Let's meet. Call
me.

'*Monday 10.21 p.m.*'

—Anne. Good evening. Let me tell you what I'm going to
do to you. First you're going to suck my cock. Then
I'm going to fuck you up the arse. With a broken bot-
tle. And that's just for starters. Little miss cunt.

'*Monday 10.30 p.m.*'

—Anne?
Pick up the phone. (*pause*) I know you're there. (*pause*)
It's no use hiding, Anne. Hiding from what? (*pause*)
The world? Hiding from the world, Anne? Come *on*.
Grow up. Grow up, Anne, and pick up the phone.
(*pause*)
So what is this then? A cry for help? Don't tell me this
is a cry for help. Because what am *I* supposed to do
exactly about *your* cry for help? Mm? (*pause*)
And what if you're lying there, Anne, already dead?
Mm?
Is that the scenario I'm supposed to imagine?
The scenario of a dead body rotting next to the
machine?

3

(faint laugh. Pause)
The what, the larvae of flies listening to your messages?
Or if your building has been destroyed.
Or if your *city* has been destroyed.
The airports and the shoe shops. The theatres and the
fashionable halogen-lit cafés that have sprung up in the
disused warehouses by the disused canals. Mm?
(faint laugh) So only the larvae of insects are listening
to your messages. Listening to me, Anne, as they tunnel
through your remains.
(pause)
I'm growing morbid, Anne.
I think you should pick up the phone and make me
smile, make me smile the way you used to, Anne.
I know you're there.
I know you're there, Anne. And I know that if I'm
patient, you'll answer me.
(pause)
You will answer me, won't you Anne.

'Tuesday 12.19 a.m.

That was your last message.
To save all messages press one.
(pause)
All messages deleted.'

4

2 TRAGEDY OF LOVE AND IDEOLOGY

—Summer. A river. Europe. These are the basic ingredients.

—And a river running through it.

—A river, exactly, running through a great European city
and a couple at the water's edge. These are the basic
ingredients.

—The woman?

—Young and beautiful, naturally.

—The man?

—Older, troubled, sensitive, naturally.

—A naturally sensitive man but nevertheless a man of
power and authority who knows that this is wrong.

—They both know this is wrong.

—They both know this is wrong but they can't / help
themselves. Exactly.

—They're making love in the man's apartment.

—Doing what?

—Making love. Making love in the man's apartment. A
luxury apartment, naturally, with a view over the entire
city. These are the / basic ingredients.

—A panorama of the entire city. The charming geometry
of the rooftops. The skylights and the quaint chimneys.
And beyond the TV aerials are monuments of culture:
the Duomo of Florence and the arch at la Défense, Nel-
son's Column and the Brandenburg Gate / to name but
four.

—The woman cries out. Her golden hair cascades as it

were over the edge of the bed. She grips the bed-frame. Her knuckles whiten. There are tears / in her eyes.

—The apartment is beautifully furnished.

—Well obviously the apartment would be beautifully furnished. Obviously it would have high ceilings and tall windows and date in all probability date from the end of the nineteenth century when the rise in speculative building coincided with the aspirations of the liberal bourgeoisie to create monumental architectural schemes such as I'm thinking particularly now I'm thinking of the Viennese Ringstrasse which made such an impression on the young Adolf Hitler as he stood one morning / before the Opera.

—Or one of the great Parisian / boulevards.

—Or one of the great, exactly, Parisian / boulevards.

—And meanwhile, as you say, her golden hair cascades as it were over the edge of the bed. She grips the frame. Her knuckles whiten and her pupils widen, while he –

—Let's say he grunts.

—Grunts?

—Let's say he grunts, yes, but sensitively. Let's say it's the sensitive grunt of the attractive man of power and authority, not for example the coarse pig-like grunt of a mechanic lying on his back in a confined space trying to loosen a cross-threaded nut with a heavy and inappropriately sized wrench.

—Absolutely not.

—Absolutely not, but the masterful grunt of a man who breakfasts on one continent and lunches on another, who flies first class with a linen napkin and a comprehensive wine list.

6

—That kind of man.

—That kind of grunt.

—That kind of light.

—What kind of light?

—The kind of light that streams in. It streams in through the tall windows transforming their bodies into a kind of golden mass.

—A writhing mass.

—The light, the golden mass, these are the / essential ingredients.

—But now a look crosses her face.

—A what?

—A look.

—A doubt.

—A look of doubt, yes, good, crosses Anne's face.

—Even now.

—Even now in the / intensity of her passion.

—Even now in the intensity of her passion a kind of shadow crosses her face.

—A premonitory shadow.

—Premonitory?

—A premonitory shadow, yes, crosses her face.

—Is that a word?

—Is what a word?

Pause.

Well yes, of course premonitory / is a word.

7

—Later. Night.

—The lights of the city at night. Strings of light suspended star-like along the quays and the frameworks of bridges. Odd dull red warning lights pulsing on the tops of tower blocks and TV transmitters. The man at the telephone. His lowered voice. His troubled glances.

—Anne wakes up in the solid walnut bed hears his faint male voice in the adjoining room. The exquisite Louis Quatorze clock beside her chimes three by means of a tiny tiny naked gilt shepherd striking a tiny tiny golden bell held between the teeth of an enamelled wolf, no doubt a reference to an ancient myth well known to the seventeenth-century French nobility but now totally erased from human consciousness.

—Ting ting ting.

Pause.

—3 a.m. Anne wakes up. Hears voice. Lights cigarette. Appears in doorway. Dialogue.

—Who was it, she says.

—Nothing, he says.

—Who the fuck was it, she says. End of dialogue.

—And now she's angry – exactly: end of dialogue – and now she's angry. She's angry because she knows exactly who it is.

—His political masters / calling him.

—His political masters, that's right, calling him. Just as they have always called him. The very political masters that she hates with every fibre as it were of her being. The very men and women, that she, Anne, in her youthful idealism holds responsible for the terminal

8

injustice of this world.

—The leaders who in her naïve and passionate opinion have destroyed everything she values in the name (a) of business and (b) of laissez-faire.

—In the name (a) of rationalization and (b) / of enterprise.

—In the name of (a) so-called individualism and (b) / of so-called choice.

—The basic ingredients in other words of a whole tragedy.

—A whole, exactly, tragedy unfolds before our eyes in Paris, Prague, Venice or Berlin to name but four, as the moon, vast and orange, rises over the renaissance domes, baroque palaces, nineteenth-century zoos and railway stations, and modernist slabs of social housing exemplifying the dictum *form follows function*.

—Form follows function.

—This whole tragedy / of love.

—This whole tragedy of ideology and love.

—She stubs out the cigarette.

—She begins to shout.

—She begins to beat him with her fists.

—She begins to bite him with her teeth.

—She begins to kick him with her bare white feet.

—She beats and beats / and beats.

—She beats and beats. And the exquisite clock which has survived two revolutions and three centuries is smashed to pieces on the smooth and highly polished parquet as she beats bites and kicks.

—The tiny tiny shepherd and the tiny tiny bell both van-

9

ish – rather a nice touch this – vanish for ever under the / walnut bed.

—Until she stops for breath. Let's say she finally, shall we, stops, at this point, for breath.

—The woman?

—The woman, Anne, yes, stops for breath.

Pause.

—And he?

—Bows his head.

—Yes.

—Looks up at her.

—Yes.

—Takes her tear-stained / face between his hands.

—Takes Anne's tear-stained face between his hands like a precious chalice.

—Or a rugby-football.

—Like a precious silver chalice or as you say a rugby-football before a drop-kick he takes Anne's angry tear-stained face between his hands.

—He still loves her.

—For all their ideological differences – that's right – he still loves her. Speech.

—One day, Anne, he says, you'll understand my world. One day, Anne, you'll understand that everything must be paid for, that even your ideals must finally be paid for. End of speech. At which he smoothes the wet strands of hair from her lips and kisses her. These are the / basic ingredients.

—He kisses her and presses her back down on to the bed. Or she him. Better still: *she* presses *him* back down on to the bed such is her emotional confusion, such is her sexual appetite, such is her inability to distinguish between right and wrong in this great consuming passion in the high-ceilinged apartment with the solid walnut bed, the polished parquet floor, the grand piano by Pleyel circa 1923 without it should perhaps be noted any visible means of protection against pregnancy in the case of Anne or in the case of either against sexually transmitted diseases including the so-called 'AIDS' virus more correctly known as the human immune-deficiency virus or / HIV for short.

—A portrait of a young girl sketching once thought to be by David but now attributed to his female contemporary Constance Charpentier, and a triangular yellow ashtray with the legend 'Ricard' containing three cigarette butts and a quantity of fine grey ash.

Pause.

—A great tragedy in other words / of love.

—A great – exactly – tragedy of ideology / and love.

—These are the basic ingredients.

Silence.

—The whole of the past is there in her face. It's written there like a history. The history of her family. The history of the land itself – this land where her family has lived for generations.

Silence.

—It's a valley.

—It's a valley – yes – deep in the hills.

—It's a valley deep in the hills where the traditional ways have been maintained for generations. And there are fruit-trees.

—Each child who is born in this valley has a fruit-tree planted in their name. In fact there's a kind of ceremony.

—A formal – exactly – ceremony.

—A kind of formal ceremony takes place in the village. And for generation upon generation this formal ceremony of naming has taken place on the birth of each child.

—The trees in other words have names.

—They have names just as the inhabitants have names. There is the person, and there is the tree. There is Anya the woman, and there is Anya the tree.

—The trees have names and so do the blades, the blades of grass. Because life is so precious, life is so *felt*, things are so *alive*, so *sacred*, that even the blades of grass have names. It's something we can hardly *comprehend*.

—We can hardly comprehend this sacred sacred life, this

sense of completeness is beyond our understanding, this sense of awe humbles us.

—But now, devastation.

Silence.

—What?

—Devastation. The harmony of generations / has been destroyed.

—Exactly. This enclosed, secure world has been torn apart.

—The harmony of generations has been destroyed. The women have been raped. The little children have been disembowelled.

—The women have been raped, and then disembowelled. The men have hacked each other to pieces.

—Brother has killed brother.

—Cousin has murdered cousin. Brother has raped sister.

—Brother has raped – yes – sister, and now the dogs are picking over the remains.

—The petrol used to fuel the ancient tractors and generate electricity for the old black-and-white TVs has been used to set people alight.

—Yes.

—First to set living people alight, and now, for health reasons, to burn the corpses.

—Living people set on fire. The cold vapour of the petrol, then the hot rush of flame. The burning people running blazing between the fruit trees which bear their names, scorching the leaves, writhing on the blades of grass, while the soldiers stand by laughing.

—The soldiers are laughing even though these are their own cousins, their own *parents*, their / mothers and fathers.

—Burning their own *parents* in the sacred orchard. Burning them alive and laughing.

—Or burying them alive. Burying them alive up to their necks in the fertile earth, then smashing their skulls open with a spade. They have a name for this.

—'The flower.'

—It's called, that's right, 'the flower'.

Silence.

And it's all there in her face.

—It's what?

—All there. All there in her face.

—In Anya's face. We don't need words. She's beyond words. Her mouth, in fact her mouth trembles but no words come.

—The inadequacy of words.

—The terrifying, yes, inadequacy of words as she stands by a tree covered in delicate white petals.

—A plum.

—A plum tree covered in delicate white petals which is the moment . . .

—Yes.

— . . . the moment we realize that *this is her tree*.

—This is *her own tree*, Anya's tree.

—Anya's tree, planted what? forty? fifty? years ago on the day of her birth. The hole dug by her father, the roots

14

spread out by her mother and watered and tended by
the family who now lie dead.

—Her very own tree.

—The air still smells of petrol.

—It's spring.

Silence.

—Panorama of the whole valley.

—The whole deep valley in spring.

—The trees. The grass.

—A bee crawls into the cup of a flower.

—And now she speaks.

—Yes. Because she *must*. Because the words well up as
she stands beside her tree.

—The tree gives her strength, the strength / to speak.

—She points to some charred timbers. That, she says, was
my home. My children were hiding under the bed.
They killed them both. First the boy. Then the girl.
They set light to my little girl's hair. I still don't know
why they set light to my little girl's hair. It crackled like
a pile of sticks.

—Then she breaks down.

—Who? Anya?

—She screams. She breaks down and scratches her cheeks
like something / from an ancient tragedy.

—I don't think so. I don't think Anya screams. I don't think
she breaks down and scratches her cheeks like something
from an ancient tragedy. I think her eyes blaze. I think
she advances towards the camera and begins to curse.

15

You mother-fucking shit-faced murderers, she says. You pig-fucking cock-sucking bastards. You sister-fucking blaspheming child-murdering mindless fuck-faced killers. I spit on your graves and on the graves of your mothers and fathers and curse all future generations.

—She's angry.

—She's very angry.

Silence.

She's very angry, but she has a *right* to be.

—She has – well obviously – a right to be angry. Everything destroyed. A way of *life* destroyed. A relationship / with *nature* destroyed.

—And this is why we sympathize.

—Of *course* we sympathize.

—Not just sympathize, but *empathize*. Empathize because . . .

—Yes.

— . . . because Anya's valley is *our* valley. Anya's trees are *our* trees. Anya's family is the family to which we all belong.

—So it's a universal thing / *obviously*.

—It's a universal thing in which we recognize, we strangely recognize ourselves. Our own world. Our own pain.

—Our own anger.

—A universal thing which strangely . . . what? what? what?

—Which strangely restores.

—Which strangely restores – I think it does – yes – our faith in ourselves.

—She's the kind of person who believes the message on the till receipt.

—'Thank you for your custom.'

—She never stands forward of this notice . . .

—Never.

— . . . or speaks to the driver.

Pause.

—When a letter comes addressed to 'The Occupier', she first of all makes . . .

—What? A cup of tea?

—Yes. Then sits at the kitchen table to open it. She opens it and reads it as carefully as if it were a letter from her own son, who now lives in America.

—Canada, actually.

—She's the kind of person who believes the lucky numbers have / been selected . . .

—Toronto.

— . . . just for her. Which in a way of course, they have. And if she replies within ten days, she will receive a mystery gift. / Toronto? Is it?

—It's not a mystery gift, no. She ticks a *box*, she ticks a *box selecting* the gift she wants to receive: maybe a handy clock-radio, a camera or a set of / miniature screwdrivers.

—A set of miniature screwdrivers or a handy disposable camera.

—She's a non-smoker.

Silence.

—She's definitely a non-smoker. Although I think it's true to say she may occasionally take cigarettes from other people.

—Exactly. At parties.

The camera *loves* you
The camera *loves* you
The camera *loves* you

We *need* to sympathize
We *need* to empathize
We *need* to advertise
We *need* to realize
We are the good guys
We are the good guys

We need to feel
what we're seeing is real
It isn't just acting
it's far more exacting
than acting
We're talking reality
We're talking humanity
We're talking of a plan to be
OVERWHELMED by the sheer totality
and utterly believable three-dimensionality
THREE-DIMENSIONALITY
of all the things that Anne can be
ALL THE THINGS THAT ANNE CAN BE

What's Hecuba to him or he to Hecuba?
A megastar
A MEGASTAR

The camera *loves* you
The camera *loves* you
The camera *loves* you

We *need* to fantasize
We *need* to improvise
We *need* to synthesize

We *need* to advertise that
We are the good guys
We are the good guys

We need to go
for the sexiest scenario
It isn't just writing
it's much more exciting
than writing
We're talking actuality
We're talking contemporary
We're saying that we want to be
OVERWHELMED by the sheer quantity
YES BY THE SHEER QUANTITY
of all the things that Anne can be
ALL THE THINGS THAT ANNE CAN BE

What's Hecuba to her or she to Hecuba?
A megastar
(A megastar? The fuck you are)

The camera loves you
The camera loves you
The camera the camera
the camera the camera
the camera the camera
THE CAMERA LOVES YOU

—It's not her first attempt.

—It shouldn't be her first attempt. She's tried at various times. Even before she leaves home / she tries, doesn't she?

—She tries at various times throughout her *life*.

—We see the other times.

—We live *through* the other times. We live through these harrowing times.

Silence.

—We see photos, don't we.

—We see large numbers of photos.

—We see them close to, so close you can make out the little dots. Funny, isn't it, how everything at a certain point turns into just these little dots – even her smile.

—It's a happy smile. It's a genuine enough smile.

—Oh yes, it's a genuinely happy / smile all right.

—Because no one's *forcing* her, no one's forcing her to smile, are they?

—No one's forcing her to do *anything*. The idea of Annie, little Annie being forced to do things is quite frankly ludicrous.

—No question of it.

Silence. In the silence:

> 'She enjoys hosting these holidays
> because she loves meeting people.
> She will introduce you to your fellow guests
> ensuring that everyone has a memorable time.'

Absolutely – and this should be made clear – absolutely no question of her doing what she does not / want to do.

—Everything at a certain point turns into these little dots – eyes, hair, smile.

—Smiles from all over the world.

—*People* from all over the world. People from all over the world photographed with Annie. Smiling with Annie. Characters I suppose who just popped in and / out of her life.

—And then popped out again.

—And then – yes – popped straight out again.

—Porno, actually, some of them.

—Porno? Come on. Hardly.

—Pretty pornographic, actually, some / of those pictures.

—I'd hardly call it pornographic, just high spirits. Just the high spirits you'd expect of a girl who's always smiling, always laughing, always on the move, always meeting someone, always leaving someone, always in a departure lounge or a bus station or waiting by an airport carousel or sleeping in the corridor / of a train.

—Always by the side of the road somewhere with that big red bag of hers. Somewhere in Africa, say, with that big red canvas bag she got from Mum and Dad when she turned sixteen. Somewhere in South America.

—Somewhere in Europe with that big / red bag.

—Europe, Africa, South America, you name it. Brazil.

—Cuba. Brazil. Romania. / *Nigeria*.

—Romania. Cuba. Florida. Australia.

—That's right. Australia. New Zealand. The / Philippines.

—Morocco. Algeria. Tunisia. The Sahara desert.

—The Kalahari desert, the foothills of the Himalayas.

—The foothills of the Alps.

—That's right – the what's it called –

—The / Piedmont.

—The Piedmont. Always in some foothills somewhere
with that big red bag of hers.

—Because, let's face it, she *is* concerned.

—Well of *course* she's concerned. We can *see* that she's
concerned. You only have to see her for example in
those photos, the way she's rubbing shoulders with the
poor. She's not afraid in those photos to rub shoulders
with the poor.

—Pictures of her in slums with the smiling slum-dwellers.

—Pictures of her on hillsides with the smiling hill-
dwellers.

—Pictures of her – exactly – with the smiling hill-dwellers
whose land has been eroded, just swept off – fwah! –
by the wind.

—And on rubbish dumps.

—Pictures of Annie on rubbish dumps next to smiling
people actually living on the dumps, actually living
right there on the dumps / with their *children*.

—Whole families of gypsies or whatever they are, are
apparently living, that's right, right there on the dumps.

—What it's not – and this is perhaps how it differs from
those previous attempts – what it's not is a cry for help.

—It's quite clear that her mind's / made up.

—It's not a cry for help. It's very important to establish that, wouldn't you agree, from the outset. It's very important to establish that no one could've helped / her at that point.

—No one could've helped her – not her Mum – not her Dad – and certainly none of her so-called / *friends*.

—She wouldn't've / *wanted* help.

—Help is the last thing she would've wanted.

Silence. In the silence:

> 'She enjoys spending lots of time with guests,
> and gets a feeling of great satisfaction
> when everyone is having a good time.
> She says there are lots of hugs at the station
> when it's time to go home, with holidaymakers
> waving and calling out
> "see you next time" from the train window.'

Laughter all through next passage:

—Some of the strange things she says . . .

—Some of the strange things she says to her Mum and Dad as a child: 'I feel like a screen.'

—'I feel like a screen.'

—She's lying there, isn't she, with the tube in her poor thin arm, looking terribly pale, whiter in fact than / the *pillow*.

—'Like a TV screen,' she says, 'where everything from the front looks real and alive, but round the back there's just dust and a few wires.'

—'Dust and a few wires.' Her imagination . . .

24

—She says she's not a real character, not a real character like you get in a book or on TV, but a *lack* of character, an *absence* she calls it, doesn't she, of character.

—An absence of character, whatever *that* means . . .

—*Then* she wants to be a terrorist, doesn't she?

—That's right. She comes down one night to the kitchen with those big earnest eyes of hers and tells her Mum and Dad she wants to be a terrorist.

—The looks on their faces . . .

—She wants her own little room and a gun and a list of names.

—'Targets.'

—A list – that's right – of so-called targets and their photographs. She wants to kill one a week then come back to the little room and drink Earl Grey tea.

—That's right – it has to be Earl Grey – and it has to be one a week.

—Her poor Mum and Dad are / *horrified*.

—They absolutely don't know how to take this.

—They've never bought Earl Grey tea / in their *lives*.

—She'd like to act like a machine, wouldn't she.

—Act? She'd like to *be* a machine. Sometimes she spends days on end, whole days on end pretending to be a television / or a car.

—A car or a television, an automatic pistol or a treadle sewing-machine.

Silence. In the silence:

'She is an excellent singles' host,

25

and loves to take people
on guided walks.'

—A sewing-machine . . . The things she comes out with . . .

—Then of course she's off round the world. One minute
it's Africa, the next it's South America or Europe.

—Somewhere in Europe.

—Europe, Africa, South America, you name it. Brazil.

—Cuba. Brazil. Romania. / *Nigeria*.

—Romania. Cuba. Florida. Australia.

—That's right. Australia. New Zealand. The / Philippines.

—Morocco. Algeria. Tunisia. The Sahara desert.

—The Kalahari desert. The foothills of the Himalayas.

—The foothills of the Alps.

—That's right – the what's it called –

—The / Piedmont.

—The Piedmont, the Piedmont, the Piedmont, of course it
is. Yes. Always some foothills somewhere with that big
red bag of hers.

—And the same hair. Don't forget the same hair down / to
her waist.

—The same long hair down to her waist at forty as she
had at twenty – like a young girl still, isn't she, in some
of / those pictures.

—Even at forty she still looks and dresses like a young girl
half her age.

—But what's really conclusive is that the bag is full of
stones.

26

—The fascinating thing, that's right, is that the bag turns out to be full / of stones.

—The stones are there to keep her under however much she thrashes, and the handles of the bag are tied to her ankles.

—No question in other words of a / cry for help.

—In other words she's planned all this, she's planned on thrashing, she knew she'd thrash, and equally she knew that the bag would go on dragging her down regardless. So there's never at any point any question of the attempt failing. There's never at any point any question of anyone being able to intervene – not Mum or Dad certainly.

—Well certainly not Mum and Dad – and certainly none of her so-called *friends*.

—If you can *call* them / friends.

—Well you obviously *can't* call them friends.

Silence. In the silence:

> 'She likes to attend keep-fit classes,
> amateur dramatics, and take part
> in lively cabarets.
> She is also a member of
> her local rambling club.'

—And we're tempted to think – aren't we – that perhaps the bag was *always* full of stones. From the moment in fact that she left the house, her Mum and Dad's house on her sixteenth birthday. Aren't we?

Pause.

Well aren't we?

—Aren't we what?

—Tempted. Tempted to imagine that maybe the bag was always full of stones from that very first day. From the moment she went down her Mum and Dad's path and closed her Mum and Dad's gate and caught the bus. That the red bag in the photographs is full of stones. That on the trucks and trains and mules she used to climb up mountains – and on the dumps and slums and hillsides and cobbled Renaissance piazzas, the bag is full of stones. And in the refugee camps where she posed at their request next to the stick-like dying just as she posed apparently without a murmur beside the Olympic swimming-pools of paunchy billionaires, the bag is full of stones. And on the airport carousels. Particularly on the airport carousels at 2 a.m. waiting with travellers from other time-zones and war-zones for the machinery to start and the luggage to appear through the black rubber curtain on the black rubber track – the rucksacks and the leather cases, the Samsonites and the taped up cardboard boxes – the bag, that red bag of hers is full of stones.

—We can't be sure.

—Well of course we can't be sure. But from what we know of her, from what we see of her, it's not / imposs-ible.

—We can't be sure that the bag is full of stones. It could be full of old clothes, drugs . . . / anything.

—Why not? Why *can't* we be sure? Why can't we say once and for all that the bag is full of stones, and that the stones explain the smile.

—The stones, it's true, would explain the smile.

—The stones would definitely explain the smile from what we've seen of her. Because there is a funny side to this.

28

—A what?

—A side. A funny side.

—Oh yes. There's definitely a funny side.

Silence. In the silence:

> 'Ann feels that there is sometimes a problem
> with the word "singles", as it is often misunderstood.
> She would like to stress that these holidays
> are not match-making events, but instead bring
> like-minded people together in informal
> and friendly surroundings,
> allowing them to enjoy a holiday together,
> and leave as friends.'

Each speech is first spoken in an African or Eastern European language. An English translation immediately follows.*

—[phrase]
—The car twists along the Mediterranean road.

—[phrase]
—It hugs the bends between the picturesque hillside villages.

—[phrase]
—The sun gleams on the aerodynamic body.

—[phrase]
—The aerodynamic body of the new *Anny*.

—[phrase]
—We see the new *Anny* snake along between the red-tiled Mediterranean rooftops.

—[phrase]
—Fast.

—[phrase]
—Sleek.

—[phrase]
—Free.

—[phrase]
—We now understand that the *Anny* comes with electric windows as standard.

—[phrase]
—We now understand that the *Anny* comes with driver's *and* passenger's airbag as standard.

*In the first production, Serbo-Croatian.

—[phrase]
—We now understand that all the things other manufacturers offer as extras . . .

—[phrase]
— . . . are offered on the *Anny* as standard.

—[phrase]
—Air-conditioning.

—[phrase]
—Engine-immobilizer.

—[phrase]
—And a mobile telephone.

—[phrase]
—We understand that our children will be safe and happy in the back seat of the *Anny* just as the adults will be relaxed and confident at the wheel.

—[phrase]
—Happy.

—[phrase]
—Secure.

—[phrase]
—In control.

—[phrase]
—The *Anny* skims the white beaches of the world as easily as she parks outside the halogen-lit shoe shops of the great cities.

—[phrase]
—When we arrive at our destination in the *Anny* . . .

—[phrase]
— . . . we will always be embraced by good-looking men and good-looking women.

—[phrase]
—We will not be betrayed.

—[phrase]
—Tortured.

—[phrase]
—Or shot.

—[phrase]
—The two-litre *Anny* achieves excellent mileage in the simulated urban cycle . . .

—[phrase]
— . . . and is also available in diesel.

—[phrase]
—As a testimony to our ongoing concern for a cleaner, greener, environment . . .

—[phrase]
— . . . there are no filthy gypsies in the *Anny*.

—[phrase]
—Not in the *Anny* nor in the sun-filled landscapes through which the *Anny* drives.

—[phrase]
—No one in the *Anny* lies cheats or steals.

—[phrase]
—Dirty bastards.

—[phrase]
—Gangsters.

—[phrase]
—Motherfuckers.

—[phrase]
—There is no room in the *Anny* for the degenerate races . . .

—[phrase]
— . . . for the mentally deficient . . .

—[phrase]
— . . . or the physically imperfect.

—[phrase]
—No room for gypsies, Arabs, Jews, Turks, Kurds, Blacks
  or any of that human scum.

—[phrase]
—We understand that zero per cent finance is available.

—[phrase]
—But hurry.

—[phrase]
—Since this is a limited offer.

—[phrase]
—The *Anny* crosses the Brooklyn Bridge.

—[phrase]
—The *Anny* crosses the Sahara.

—[phrase]
—The *Anny* streaks through the vineyards of Bordeaux.

—[phrase]
—The *Anny* streaks at dawn through North African villages . . .

—[phrase]
—Fast.

—[phrase]
—Sleek.

—[phrase]
—Free.

—[phrase]

— . . . where the veiled women can only gaze with wonder at the immaculate rust-protected paintwork with its five-year warranty.

—[phrase]
—No one ever packs the *Anny* with explosives to achieve a political objective.

—[phrase]
—No man ever rapes and kills a woman in the *Anny* before tipping her body out at a red light along with the contents of the ashtray.

—[phrase]
—No one is ever dragged from the *Anny* by an enraged mob.

—[phrase]
—No child's pelvis is ever shattered by a chance collision with the new *Anny*.

—[phrase]
—The back seat is never made slippery by sperm.

—[phrase]
—Slippery by blood.

—[phrase]
—Slippery by beer.

—[phrase]
—Slippery by saliva.

—[phrase]
—Or sticky by melted chocolate.

—[phrase]
—Melted chocolate. Yum yum yum.

Small print:

—[phrase]

—On the road price includes VAT, number plates, delivery and six months' road fund licence.

—[phrase]

—Financial packages subject to status.

—[phrase]

—Smoking can harm your unborn child.

—[phrase]

—Your house is at risk if you do not keep up the repayments on a loan.

—I'll tell you what: she has a kind of ashtray. The tall kind on a stalk. Like something you'd find in the lobby of a cheap hotel, the kind of hotel you visit for a few hours on a weekday afternoon in a strange city with a man you've / only just met.

—With a man you'll never see again

—With a man – exactly – you've only just met and have no intention of ever seeing again. That's the kind of ashtray it is, with its chromium bowl and its chromium stalk and its aura of sudden unprotected sex in cheap hotel rooms.

—She also speaks five languages and with the aid of the CERN accelerator in Geneva has discovered a new elementary particle which will bear her name and completely change the way we look at the universe.

—She doesn't seem to care. She has no conscience. She expresses no remorse. She says, 'I do not / recognize your authority.'

—'I do not recognize your authority.' Just what does she *mean* by that? Who does she think she *is*? Does she really imagine she won't have to account for the lives she's destroyed? Does she really imagine that anything can justify her acts of random senseless violence? Nothing in her eyes reveals one spark / of human feeling.

—Not one spark – that's right – of human feeling or any sense of shame. Is this the same child, is this the same child who once wore a pink gingham dress and a straw hat and went with the daughters of doctors, dentists, TV presenters and property developers to the school on the hill with the polished brass plate and the teachers in strict tartan skirts? Is this the same child who had Fantasy Barbie™, Fantasy Ken™ and all the outfits: the tiny tiny knickers and the tiny tiny shoes? The house, the horse, and Barbie's™ / very own car?

—Is this the same little Anne who put all the tiny tiny shoes in rows and all the tiny tiny dolls in rows and all the tiny tiny beads in rows and what's more prayed to God™ each night / with no sense whatsoever of irony.

—Who prayed to God™ 'God™ bless Mummy, God™ bless Daddy, God™ bless Wiggy the cat, God™ bless everyone' with no sense whatsoever of irony but rather in the sincere belief that she might invoke there on her knees and in her Minnie Mouse™ pyjamas the blessing of the Father and of the Son / and of the Holy Ghost.

—Amen.

—Who wet the bed each and every night until her sleepless parents took her to the doctor with his heap of magazines to pull with a big smile down her knickers on the high cold leather couch and say, 'Let's take a look then, Anne, / shall we'?

—The same Anne who came away from the hospital with a wooden box containing a bell to go beside the bed, two stiff squares of metal gauze and a number / of black wires?

—The same Anne who woke up each subsequent night to the sound of the horrible bell in the horrible / wet sheets?

—The same Anne who now – what? – *stands* there? *Stands* there in front of serious men and women with witnesses and evidence in sealed plastic bags – false passports and pieces of human flesh – who stands there and refuses / to recognize their *authority*?

—Pieces of human flesh, false passports, lists of names, traces of explosive, tapes of phone-calls, videotapes from banks and shopping malls and cash dispensers. Psychiatric reports which confirm (a) her intelligence and (b) her sanity. 'She set about her work,' they say, 'with all the terrible detachment of an artist.' Witnesses break down / in tears.

—Witnesses break down in tears as videotapes from banks and shopping malls show Anne as just one more person going about their business under constant surveillance, until twenty minutes after she's left, the plate glass blows out of a shoe-shop window in absolute silence and the little grey figures breaking apart and flying through the air in absolute silence with the tiny tiny flying shoes are real human beings mixed with glass. No one can find out / what her motive is.

38

—No one can find Anne's motive.

—She lives alone?

—She lives alone.

—She works alone?

—She works alone.

—She sleeps alone?

—Apparently, yes.

—Kills / alone? Eats?

—She lives works sleeps kills and eats entirely on her own. In fact her recorded phone-calls consist almost entirely of orders for meals to be delivered to the rooms she rented overlooking the highstreets of metro- politan suburbs – a large pizza, garlic bread, and one and a half litres of Diet Pepsi™ all for just nine pounds / ninety-nine.

—Calls which are at first assumed to be / coded messages.

—Calls which are at first, that's right, assumed to be coded messages but which are simply orders for meals delivered to her door by boys on scooters and / paid for in cash.

—Is this really the same little Anne who now has wit- nesses breaking down in tears? Who now has long- serving officers of both sexes receiving counselling for the night-sweats, impotence, amenorrhea, trembling hands and flashbacks of human heads popping open as if in slow motion and the long long terrible wail of a buried unreachable child recurring as a kind of what's the word?

—An auditory hallucination?

—Yes. For which they're now demanding / to be *compensated*.

—The same Anne who woke up when the bell went and watched the shadows of the chestnut trees move on her bedroom wall in her / wet pyjamas?

—The same Anne who soldered fiddly timing mechanisms and mercury tilt-switches to printed circuit boards with her mouth full of / deep-pan pizza?

—Who summed up the mood / of a generation.

—Who appeared twice on the cover of / Vogue™ magazine.

—Who sold the film rights for two and a half million / US dollars.

—Who studied in depth the baggage-handling procedures and memorized the timetables of the principal international / airlines.

—Who was quote a loner / unquote.

—Who listens quote expressionlessly unquote to the description of quote outrage unquote after quote outrage unquote after quote outrage unquote she has perpetrated.

—It's kinda funny and it's kinda sad.
I guess it's kinda bittersweet.
I guess it's one of these kinda bittersweet things, one of
these laughing through *tears* things.
After so much time, after so many years, he finally
comes back to his Mom.
And at first, y'know, like 'Who *is* this?'
Then there's the moment of realization: 'Oh *God*: it's
my very own son.'

And they're hugging each other right there in the
kitchen and y'know that is so *moving*.
I mean that is just so moving to see that he has found
that thing, that *strength*, to forgive his Mom.
That he has forgiven her her *alcoholism*.
That he has forgiven her for running round with other
men.
That he has forgiven her for destroying his father's
faith in himself and driving him to *suicide*.
And they're both kinda crying and laughing and crying
again all at the same time in the same kitchen he sat in
as a little boy witnessing his parents' terrible argu-
ments. His Dad in tears pouring her liquor down the
sink at ten o'clock in the morning while she screams
how if he was a real man with one iota of self-respect
she wouldn't need to booze herself to death, would she.
And there are these tiny scratches in the table which he
recalls having made secretly with a fork. And you're
aware, y'know, like of the *continuity* of things, of the
bittersweetness of things.

And then he says, 'Hey, Mom, I have a surprise for
you.' And Mom kinda breaks away and wipes her eyes
and says, 'What surprise?'

And he says, 'Look out the window, Mom.'
And out the window there's like this dusty pick-up with two tiny tiny kids in the back like kinda staring. Just staring into the camera
And she can hardly believe these are her very own grandchildren.
Then he says, 'Mom, I want you to meet Annie.'

And that's when this woman Annie gets out of the pick-up and she's like real tall and fair and strong-limbed with these clear blue eyes that look right into your heart, and she's like – well I guess she's like every man's *dream* of what a good woman should be, and every mother's dream of the wife she would choose for her boy.

And it turns out how he and Annie and the kids are making this new what? Well, *life*. They are making this new, yes, life for themselves away from the city. Living off the land. Growing stuff. Trapping stuff. Boring under the earth for clean pure water. Educating their own *children*. In the belief that Man is free before God to forge his own destiny and take whatever means necessary to protect his family.

And over lunch – which is basically a kind of chicken salad with mayonnaise – we learn how he is in fact the commanding officer of a whole *group* of like-minded individuals who have armed themselves not out of any thirst for blood, but out of *necessity* because it is war. 'War?' says Mom. 'How d'you mean, war?'

So Annie has to explain to Mom how they don't believe in taxes or welfare or any of that shit. How the war is a war against a government that takes the bread out of the working-man's mouth and gives it to the pornographers and abortionists of this world.
Is a war against the God-forsaken *faggots*.

Is a war against the crack dealers and the Blacks.
Is a war against the conspiring *Jews* and their attempts
to rewrite *history*.
Is a *crusade* against the degenerate images which masquerade as *art*.
Is a war against all those who would deny our right to
bear arms.

And Annie has like this inner light.
It's like wow, she's cut, she's cut, she's cut through all
the confusion and chattering voices of our lives and of
our time and found just this kinda really what?
Thing I guess.
This thing, this like absolute *thing*.
It's like she's found this thing.
It's like – hey – Annie has found this thing, this *key*,
yes, this key thing, this secret, this certainty and simplicity, this secret and simple thing we all search for
throughout our lives and which is, I guess, the *truth*.

Yes. And it's kinda moving to see how attentive *he* is to
the kids.
How he's the one who cuts up their chicken and wipes
their mouths with a paper napkin – the image, y'know,
of this big guy in camouflage doing all that caring
domestic stuff.
'Cos family is at the heart of things, I guess.

And one of the tiny tiny children looks up from his
chicken and says, 'Daddy, why is she *crying*?'
And it's true.
His mother is crying.
As she sits there at the family table gazing on this family she never knew she had – the son and his fine young
wife, their strong and innocent children with their
whole lives ahead of them – she is, yes indeed, crying
her eyes out like a tiny child herself.

43

And Annie strokes the boy's hair – which is clipped real short, y'know – like a real young soldier – and says, 'Because she is so happy, son. Because she is so happy.'

—What we see here are various objects associated with
the artist's attempts to kill herself over the past few
months. For example: medicine bottles, records of hospital admissions, polaroids of the several HIV positive
men with whom she has had intentionally unprotected
intercourse, pieces of broken glass . . .

—Suicide notes.

— . . . yes, and the walls of the gallery have of course
been lined with her many suicide notes. In addition to
the polaroids there are rather *unpleasant*, I have to say,
video recordings of the attempts themselves.
Well I don't know about other people, but after a few
minutes of this I rather began to wish she'd succeeded
the first time round.

Silence. In the silence:

head
green
water
to sing
death
long
ship
to pay
window
friendly
table
to ask
cold
stem
to dance
village

lake
sick
pride
to cook

—Well I think that's an inexcusably frivolous comment to make about what is clearly a landmark work. It's moving. It's timely. It's distressing. It's funny. It's sick. It's sexy. It's deeply serious. It's entertaining. It's illuminating. It's dark. It's highly personal and at the same time raises vital questions about the world we're living in.

—What fascinates me is her use of textures. I think there's a great sensitivity here in the juxtaposition of materials: leather and glass, blood and paper, Vaseline and steel, which evoke in the viewer an almost / visceral reaction.

—I'm afraid what we're seeing here is pure narcissism. And I think we have to ask ourselves the question, who would possibly accept this kind of undigested exhibitionism as a work of art? . . .

—Yes, but exactly, that's surely the very point she's attempting to make: *Where* are the boundaries? *What* is acceptable? . . .

— . . . because it's pure / self-indulgence.

— . . . Where does the 'life' – literally in this case – end, and the 'work' begin?

—With respect to you I think she'd find the whole concept of 'making a point' ludicrously outmoded. If *any* point is being made at all it's *surely* the point that the point that's being made is *not* the point and never has in fact *been* the point. It's surely the point that a search for a point is pointless and that the whole point of the exercise – i.e. these attempts on her own life – *points* to

46

that. It makes me think of the Chinese proverb: the darkest place is always under the lamp.

Silence. In the silence:

ink
angry
needle
to swim
journey
blue
lamp
to sin
bread
rich
tree
to prick
pity
yellow
mountain
· to die
salt
new
custom
to pray

—The what?

—The darkest place. It's / Chinese.

—*Why* can't people learn to draw? *Why* can't people learn to paint? Students should be taught *skills*, not ideas. Because what we see here is the work of a girl who quite clearly should've been admitted not to an art school but to a psychiatric unit.

Silence. In the silence:

money
stupid
exercise-book
to despise
finger
dear
bird
to fall
book
unjust
frog
to part
hunger
white
child
to pay attention
pencil
sad
plum
to marry

—A *what*?

—A mental hospital. Somewhere where she could / receive treatment.

—Well I have to say I think that's an extraordinary remark which I would not expect to hear outside of a police-state . . .

—Oh *please* . . .

— . . . and which – no, I'm sorry, I'm sorry, this has to be said – which appears to be an attempt to reinstate the notion of *Entartete Kunst* . . .

—Oh rubbish. What an absurd / over-reaction.

— . . . the so-called 'degenerate art' prohibited – rubbish?

I don't think so – prohibited by the Nazis. I mean *listen* to yourself: you are saying that this artist should not be allowed to produce work but should instead be compelled to undergo psychiatric treatment.

—I'm simply suggesting that this poor girl . . .

—'This poor girl.'

— . . . this poor girl, yes, requires help – and I have not as you well know at any point suggested that she should be / 'compelled'.

—Requires help? Oh really? And in whose opinion? The opinion of Goebbels? The opinion perhaps of Joseph Stalin? Isn't Anne actually anticipating the terrifying consequences of that argument and asking us what 'help' actually means? Isn't she saying, 'I don't want your help'? Isn't she saying, 'Your help oppresses me'? Isn't she saying the only way to avoid being a victim of the patriarchal structures of late twentieth-century capitalism is to *become her own victim*?
Isn't that the true meaning of these attempts on her life?

—Her own victim – that's fascinating.

—Oh really, this is such flabby reasoning.

Silence. In the silence:

house
darling
glass
to quarrel
fur
big
carrot
to paint
part

old
flower
to beat
box
wild
family
to wash
cow
friend
happiness
lie

—Well I think whatever the very varied personal agendas
we bring to this, we're all agreed that it's a landmark
work. It's moving. It's timely. It's distressing. It's funny.
It's sick. It's sexy. / It's deeply serious. It's entertaining.
It's cryptic. It's dark. It's highly personal and at the
same time raises vital questions about the world we're
living in.

—(*cue 'sexy'*) That really is such flabby reasoning. Her
own victim? If she really is – as it appears – trying to
kill herself, then surely our presence here makes us
mere voyeurs in Bedlam. If on the other hand she's only
play-acting, then the whole work becomes a mere cyni-
cal performance and is doubly disgusting.

—But why not? Why shouldn't it be / 'a performance'?

—Exactly – it becomes a kind / of theatre.

—It's theatre – that's right – for a world in which theatre
itself has died. Instead of the outmoded conventions of
dialogue and so-called characters lumbering towards
the embarrassing dénouements of the *theatre*, Anne is
offering us a pure dialogue of objects: of leather and
glass, of Vaseline and steel; of blood, saliva and chocolate. She's offering us no less than the spectacle of her

own existence, the radical *pornography* – if I may use that overused word – of her own broken and abused – almost *Christ*-like – body.

—An object in other words. A *religious* object.

—An object, yes. But not the object of *others*, the object of *herself*. *That's* the scenario / she offers.

—But surely we've seen all that. Haven't we seen all that in the so-called 'radicalism' of the sixties stroke seventies?

Silence. In the silence:

> deportment
> narrow
> brother
> to fear
> stork
> false
> anxiety
> to kiss
> bride
> pure
> door
> to choose
> hay
> contented
> ridicule
> to sleep
> month
> nice
> woman
> abuse

—*Seen* it – perhaps. But not seen it afresh, not seen it now, not seen it in the context of a *post*-radical, of a post-*human* world where the *gestures* of radicalism take on new meaning in a society where the radical gesture is simply one more form of entertainment i.e. one more product – in this case an artwork – to / be consumed.

—Theatre has nothing to do with this and I bitterly resent the implication that I am some kind of a *Nazi*.

Silence.
—STRANGELY!
Silence.

—She is nineteen, has a long braid of glossy mahogany hair, and holds a silver stop-watch.

He has a thick beard, a family, and a list of one hundred words.

He says: 'Anna, I love you.'

She says: 'But Karl, you are married.'

He takes her hand and begins to suck her ringless fingers, right down to the root.

She says: 'I walked today for the first time along the Limmat, on the lonely path that runs parallel to Promenadenstrasse. It was especially wonderful to look through the branches of those great old trees that bend almost down to the rushing water.'

Silence.

She's the girl next door
She's the fatal flaw
She's the reason for
The Trojan War.

She is royalty
She practices art
She's a refugee
In a horse and cart.

She's a pornographic movie star
A killer and a brand of car
A KILLER AND A BRAND OF CAR!

She's a terrorist threat
She's a mother of three
She's a cheap cigarette
She is Ecstasy.

She's a femme fatale
She's the edge of the knife
She's one helluva gal
She's Intelligent Life.

She's a presidential candidate
For every little warring state
EVERY LITTLE WARRING STATE!

She winters in the south
She collects antiques
She has a big mouth
But she never speaks.

She's given a spade
At the edge of a wood

To dig her own grave
By a man in a hood.

She drives a tank
Over neonates
While choosing to bank
At competitive rates.

She bombs by stealth
Has unlimited wealth
White knobbly knees.
WHAT? KNOBBLY KNEES?
Yes. Knobbly knees
And speaks fluent Japanese.

O-shigoto wa nan desu ka?
Oku-san wa imasu ka?
OKU-SAN WA IMASU KA?

She's an artificial tan
She's the fat in the pan
She's the film in the can
She's the shit in the fan.

She's the one who ran
When the shooting began.

She's a girl with a plan
She's a boy with a man
She's a dyke with a *femme*
She's a man with a van.

She's a dedicated football fan
With limited attention span
LIMITED ATTENTION SPAN!

She's the predator
She's the god of war
She's the fatal flaw

She's the girl she's the girl
She's the girl she's the girl
She's the girl she's the girl
SHE'S THE GIRL NEXT DOOR!

Silence.

—You say she rides her bike in all weathers?

—All weathers. That's right.

Silence.

—And wears a hat.

—Yes. She wears a hat.

—Which, you state, she has knitted herself.

—I believe so.

Silence.

—She grows tomato plants in . . .

—Margerine tubs.

—Margerine tubs.

—That's right.

Silence.

Or yoghurt . . .

—Yoghurt pots.

—Yes.

—I see.

Silence.

Why do you think she does that?

—What? Grow tomato plants?

—Yes.

Silence.

—For fêtes.

—For what?

—Fêtes. She sells them at fêtes.

—Of course. And I suppose she takes them to the fêtes on her bike.

—Yes she does.

—In all weathers.

—Yes she does.

—In a cardboard box.

—Yes she does.

—Now why do you suppose she does that? Why do you suppose she takes these, what, these tomato plants in yoghurt pots, why do you suppose she takes them on her bike in a cardboard box to fêtes in all weathers?

Long silence.

You state quote as a child she often shared a bed with two or three of her younger siblings unquote. Do you abide by that statement?

—Yes.

—Why?

—Because she did.

—'Because she did.'

—Because she did, yes. Because they were poor. Because they had nothing.

—Different world, eh?

Silence.

If you could just sign here.

—What?

—Yes. If you could just sign here to say you have read the statement, and consider it accurate.

Silence.

Well, don't you consider it accurate?

—If I could have a pen . . .

A pen is produced, the cap removed. The paper is signed and passed back. Silence.

Is that all?

—For the time being. Thank you.

Silence.

Thank you very much.

Silence.

The principal speaker is a very young woman. As she speaks her words are translated dispassionately into an African, South American or Eastern European language.*

—The best years of her life are ahead of her.
—[translation]

—She may be seventeen or eighteen . . .
—[translation]

— . . . but ideally she's younger . . .
—[translation]

— . . . fourteen perhaps or younger still.
—[translation]

—It's really really important to understand that she is in control.
—[translation]

—She's always in control of everything that happens.
—[translation]

—Even when it looks violent or dangerous.
—[translation]

—Which it is not.
—[translation]

—(*faint laugh*) Obviously.
—[translation]

—(*faint laugh*) Of course there's no *story* to speak of . . .
—[translation]

— . . . or characters.

*In the first production, Portuguese.

—[translation]

—Certainly not in the conventional sense.
—[translation]

—But that's not to say that skill isn't required.
—[translation]

—Since we still need to feel that what we're seeing is real.
—[translation]

—It isn't just acting.
—[translation]

—It's actually far more exacting than acting – for the simple reason that it's really happening.
—[translation]

*A pause. She seems to have forgotten what to say and
looks for a prompt.*

—Yes?
—(*prompt*) She enjoys her work.
—What?
—(*more emphatic prompt*) She enjoys her work.
—She enjoys her work.
—[translation]

—She's young and fit, and happy with her body.
—[translation]

—How she uses her body is her decision.
—[translation]

—Obviously.
—[translation]

—Porno doesn't stop her leading a normal life.
—[translation – *in the translation 'Porno' should have a
   distinctive stress: 'Pornó'*]

—She has a regular boyfriend . . .

66

—[translation]

— . . . and all the normal interests of a girl of her age.
—[translation]

—(*faint laugh*) Clothes.
—[translation]

—Boys.
—[translation]

—Make-up. Pets.
—[translation]

—Music.
—[translation]

—The difference is . . .
—[translation]

— . . . is that Porno is building up for her the kind of
  security and independence many women would envy.
—[translation]

—Porno . . .
—[translation]

— . . . is actually a way of taking control.
—[translation]

—Porno . . .
—[translation]

— . . . is actually the reverse of what it seems.
—[translation]

—Because rather than *consuming* the images . . .
—[translation]

— . . . she is producing them.
—[translation]

—That, for her, is one of the beauties of Porno.

67

—[translation]

Again a pause. She seems to have forgotten what to say: but this should imply a distress which is never allowed to surface. She looks for a prompt.

—Yes?
—(*prompt*) She is not insensitive to the evening light.
—What?
—(*more emphatic prompt*) She is not insensitive / to the evening light.
—She is not insensitive to the evening light when it strikes the tops of the pine trees with brilliant orange.
—[translation]

—She has an inner life.
—[translation]

—She responds sensitively to the world.
—[translation]

—The scenario in fact of the drugged and desensitized child . . .
—[translation]

— . . . humiliated . . .
—[translation]

— . . . and then photographed or filmed without her knowledge . . .
—[translation]

— . . . is a ludicrous caricature.
—[translation]

Again a pause. Again she looks for a prompt.

—Yes?
—(*prompt*) Everything is provided.
—What?

—(*more emphatic prompt*) Everything is provided for her needs.

Pause.

—I can't.
—[translation of 'I can't']

Pause.

—I can't
—[translation of 'I can't']

She turns away. Momentary confusion. But then another speaker takes over. In fact the rest of the company have probably appeared and may share the following lines, while the first girl drinks a glass of water and is revived; again it should not be clear whether she's suffering stage-fright or true distress.

The translator remains impassive.

—Everything is provided for her needs. Including a regular education.
—[translation]

—By age twenty-one the best years of her life will still be ahead of her . . .
—[translation]

— . . . *and* she'll have money in the bank from Porno.
—[translation]

—Not everyone has this start in life.
—[translation]

—Or her opportunities.
—[translation]

—Obviously.
—[translation]

The young woman gradually begins to join in again, supported by the other voices.

—She could for example become a model . . .
—[translation]

— . . . a TV personality . . .
—[translation]

— . . . run her own country pub or travel the world.
—[translation]

—She could paint . . .
—[translation]

— . . . swim professionally . . .
—[translation]

— . . . or study for a degree in chemical engineering.
—[translation]

All with growing élan.

—Anne could change the world . . .
—[translation]

— . . . end animal suffering . . .
—[translation]

— . . . end human suffering . . .
—[translation]

— . . . and learn to fly helicopters.
—[translation]

Passionate gypsy violin music begins.

—Anne will distribute the world's resources evenly across the earth . . .
—[translation]

— . . . raise from the dust the faces of the disaffected . . .

—[translation]

— . . . while guaranteeing not to erode the privileges of
the middle class.
—[translation]

—She will popularize psycho-analytic theory . . .
—[translation]

— . . . by probing the roots of human behaviour . . .
—[translation]

— . . . in a series of weekly magazine articles.
—[translation]

The music intensifies.

—Anne has seen the world from space . . .
—[translation]

— . . . the wrinkles of the mountains . . .
—[translation]

— . . . and the cobalt threads of the rivers.
—[translation]

—She has excavated the shallow graves . . .
—[translation]

— . . . and picked over the shattered skulls of the dead.
—[translation]

—She has scattered information in the optic fibres . . .
—[translation]

— . . . and danced with the particles of light.
—[translation]

Music intensifies. The speakers divide, creating two simul-
taneous strands, each strand impassively translated into a
different language:

—Anne has hosed down the
streets of Bucharest . . .
—[translation]

— . . . and listened to the
foetal heart.
—[translation]

—She has melted with the
ice-caps . . .
—[translation]

— . . . and flowed into the
fertile deltas.
—[translation]

—She has personally
endorsed a brand of
imported lager.
—[translation]

—She has bought an entire
newspaper page . . .
—[translation]

— . . . to print a full and
unreserved apology.
—[translation]

—She has exterminated gypsies . . .
—[translation]

— . . . and bought a sprig of
lucky heather.
—[translation]

—She has hung on a cross to
die . . .
—[translation]

—Anne will now demonstrate
the crash position . . .
—[translation]

— . . . which you should
adopt when instructed by
the stewards . . .
—[translation]

—Head down.
—[translation]

—Knees drawn up.
—[translation]

—If oxygen is required . . .
—[translation]

— . . . oxygen masks will
drop down automatically.
—[translation]

—Pull on the mask to start
the oxygen.
—[translation]

—Do not smoke while oxy-
gen is in use.
—[translation]

—Please ensure that your
seatbelt is fastened . . .
—[translation]

— . . . your table is folded
away . . .
—[translation]

— . . . risen on the third day
from the dead . . .
—[translation]

— . . . grown a beard . . .
—[translation]

— . . . and entered Mecca in
triumph.
—[translation]

—Anne will save us from the
anxiety of our century . . .
—[translation]

— . . . and usher in an age
in which the spiritual and
the material . . .
—[translation]

— . . . the commercial and
the trivial . . .
—[translation]

— . . . the wave and the
particle . . .
—[translation]

— . . . will finally be
reconciled!
—[translation]

— . . . and that your seat is
in an upright position.
—[translation]

—During the flight . . .
—[translation]

— . . . we will be coming
round with a list of duty-
free goods.
—[translation]

—Anne will save us from the
anxiety of our century . . .
—[translation]

— . . . and usher in an age in
which the spiritual and
the material . . .
—[translation]

— . . . the commercial and
the trivial . . .
—[translation]

— . . . the wave and the
particle . . .
—[translation]

— . . . will finally be
reconciled!
—[translation]

—Okay, so there's a lot on her mind. Things have . . .

—Well that's right.

— . . . things have what? Things have *changed* for her over the past few years.

—Well that's absolutely right.

—I mean we can see – let's face it: we can see that something has died.

—Something has what?

—Has died. Something / has died.

—She feels she's failed.

—Exactly. She feels her work's failed.

—But also personally – her work, yes – but also personally she feels that something, something inside of her has died.

—And *has* it?

—What?

—And *has* it died?

—Has what died?

—This thing, this so-called thing inside of her.

—What so-called thing?

—The thing, the thing, the thing, the thing / inside of her.

—In her case, yes, let's say it *has* died. Let's say that everything she's ever worked for – her whole life – has died. (*laughter*) Let's say her life up to this point has been what? what? what? like a . . .

74

—Book?

—Like a book, like a . . .

—Thread?

—Like a book, like a thread, like a . . .

—Boat?

—Like a boat. Let's say her whole life – yes, very good – up to this point has been like a boat, like a small boat . . .

—Drifting.

— . . . drifting quite happily across a lake. But now she feels the water . . .

—Coming in through the cracks?

—Creeping.

—Creeping into what?

—Her broken heart.

Laughter.

—Her broken – exactly – yes – absolutely – heart. She feels the water of the lake creeping into her / broken heart.

—Her *work* abandoned. Her *home* abandoned by her children.

—Her*self* abandoned by her *husband*. Where is *he* now?

—Paris? Prague? / Vienna? Berlin?

—Paris? Prague? Fucking? Fucking is he someone half her age in a city of Renaissance palaces and baroque / domes? Enacting some adolescent fantasy, while she attempts to reconstruct her life.

—But she never had a husband.

—She never what?

—Never had a husband. She never believed in marriage.

—Okay. Perhaps she never believed in it, but she had a husband all the same.

Laughter.

—Paul.

—Who?

—Paul.

—Paul? Paul wasn't her *husband*.

Laughter.

—Well who was he then?

—I don't know. He was just some kind of, some kind of, some kind of . . . / person.

—Like smoking.

—What? Exactly. Yes. Like smoking cigarettes.

Silence.

—Talking of which, d'you know she still has that tall ashtray on a stalk?

—Talking of what?

—Of which. Talking of which.

—She doesn't.

—She does. She still carries it round with her from / room to room.

—It's a ghastly thing.

—It is not a ghastly thing.

—It's like something out of
the lobby of a cheap
hotel, the kind of hotel
you visit for a few hours
on a weekday afternoon
in a strange city with a
man you've / only just
met.

—With a man you'll never
see again.

—With a man – exactly –
you've only just met and
have no intention of ever
seeing again. With its
chromium bowl and its
chromium stalk and its
aura of sudden unpro-
tected sex in cheap hotel
rooms. A cuspidor?
What's that?

—It is. It's like a *spittoon*.
Or what's that other
thing?

—What thing is that?

—That thing. That word.
That other word.

—What? For spittoon?

—Humidor?

—No. Not humidor, but like
it.

Pause.

—Cuspidor?

—Cuspidor. That's it. It's
like a cuspidor.

—A thing. A thing you spit in.

—She doesn't spit. What are you talking about? She
doesn't marry. She doesn't have children. And she certainly / doesn't spit.

—No one's saying she spits.

—So why then does she have a thing you spit in?

—She doesn't have a thing you spit in, she has a thing that
/ resembles one.

—But in that case, what's a humidor?

—Humidor is Spanish. Like matador.

77

—Like conquistador.

—It's a box where you / keep cigars.

—It's a box – that's right – where you keep cigars.

Silence.

—So. What? She doesn't work?

—She *does* work.

—She *has* worked.

—She *can* work.

—She *will* work.

—She *won't* work.

—What?

—She won't work.

—But she has skills.

—Oh yes, she has skills but whatever skills she has seem inappropriate to the world she's living in. Whatever *work* she's done seems inappropriate to the world she's living in. All she can do is pace round the ashtray or pull down books at random from the bookshelves.

—Don't tell me: classic texts.

—That's right – the classic texts she should've read as a student twenty or thirty years ago.

—And just like twenty or thirty years ago gets no further than the introductions.

Laughter.

—The bits she underlined with a shaky black biro . . .

—Those bits – exactly – that she underlined in biro because she thought they had some what? Some *meaning*?

—Or was taught.

—Or was what?

—Taught. Not necessarily thought, but taught. Taught they had / some meaning.

—Well – thought, taught, whatever, the fact remains she'd rather skim.

—Okay, you mean to skim seems more appropriate to the world / she's living in?

—That's exactly what I mean: she'd rather skim. She'd rather read just the smallest parts of things. Part of a recipe. Part of a letter. Part of / an article.

—Part of a recipe. Part of a letter replying to a letter she's never read about an article she missed.

—What article was that?

—She missed it.

—She missed it – okay – but we can still imagine what she might've missed.

—That thing about the actor.

—That thing about the politician.

—That thing about the fresh salmon.

—That thing about the killer. How he'd inflicted a total of 37 stab-wounds on the child's mother as the child slept.

—What thing was that?

—The salmon?

—And it was his own child.

—Yes.

—No, it wasn't his own child. But his own child was there.

—Well about how you define the word 'fresh'. What the word 'fresh' in a phrase like 'fresh salmon' actually means.

—He brought his child to watch.

—He brought his own child – that's right – to watch him murder this other child's mother.

—You mean can it mean 'previously frozen'?

—Exactly.
He did *what*?

—Brought his own child. Brought his own child in his pyjamas to watch him do it. Stab her. Yes.

Silence.

—And *can* it?

—Can it what?

—Mean 'previously frozen'?

Silence.